Early
SPACE
Encyclopedias

THE NIGHT SKY

by Tammy Gagne

Early Encyclopedias

An Imprint of Abdo Reference
abdobooks.com

abdobooks.com

Published by Abdo Reference, a division of ABDO, PO Box 398166, Minneapolis, Minnesota 55439.

Printed in China.
102025
012026

Editor: Arnold Ringstad
Series Designers: Candice Keimig, Joshua Olson
Production Designer: Ryan Gale

Library of Congress Control Number: 2025939295

Publisher's Cataloging-in-Publication Data

Names: Gagne, Tammy, author.
Title: The night sky / by Tammy Gagne
Description: Minneapolis, Minnesota: Abdo Reference, 2026 | Series: Early space encyclopedias | Includes online resources and index.
Identifiers: ISBN 9781098298791 (lib. bdg.) | ISBN 9798384932598 (ebook)
Subjects: LCSH: Outer space--Exploration--Juvenile literature. | Astronomy--Juvenile literature. | Solar System--Juvenile literature. | Night--Juvenile literature. | Sky--Juvenile literature. | Stars--Juvenile literature. | Encyclopedias--Juvenile literature.
Classification: DDC 523.8--dc23

CONTENTS

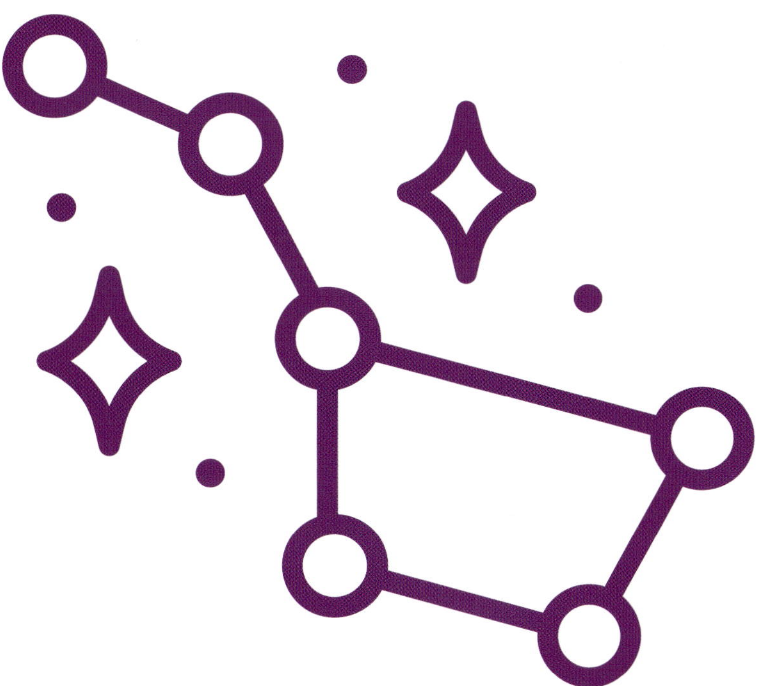

Looking at the night sky is a popular hobby.

Astonishing Objects

The sky puts on a show each night. It is filled with celestial objects. People can see stars, the moon, and planets. Some people look with just their eyes. Others use tools that reveal distant things.

A Long History

Humans have gazed at the night sky for thousands of years. Early people saw patterns in the stars. They noticed the moon's changing shape. And they saw bright lights blazing across the sky.

Ancient people used the changing appearance of the moon to help keep track of time.

Early Astronomers

The ancient Babylonians tracked the way planets move. The ancient Egyptians built pyramids to line up with stars. Early Chinese astronomers recorded where they saw the stars. People studied the sky and learned more each night.

The Babylonians recorded their discoveries on clay tablets more than 2,000 years ago.

Modern Stargazers

People still look to the stars. Many enjoy spotting familiar star patterns. Some wonder about distant galaxies. Viewing the night sky can help people feel connected to the universe.

Stargazers pick the best times to look at the night sky.

The Naked Eye

Stargazers are people who look at objects in the night sky. It is easiest to stargaze when the moon is dark. A darker night makes more space objects visible.

FUN FACT!

Looking directly at the sun is dangerous. But people can safely look at any night sky object.

Far from Cities

Stargazing is easier in the country than in the city. City lights brighten the sky. People in a large city may see only a dozen stars. People in the countryside may see more than 1,000.

Few stars are visible above brightly lit cities.

What Are Binoculars?

Binoculars help people see faraway objects. They have shaped pieces of glass called lenses. The lenses make distant objects look bigger. People look through binoculars with both eyes.

Powerful binoculars may sit on a support to keep them stable.

Binoculars provide a wider view than telescopes.

Using Binoculars

People can see more objects in the night sky by using binoculars. A star cluster is a group of stars. It may look like one star to the naked eye. Binoculars reveal the separate stars.

Early telescopes changed the way people thought about the night sky.

Early Telescopes

To see even more, people use telescopes. Dutch eyeglass maker Hans Lippershey invented the telescope in 1608. A year later, astronomer Galileo Galilei built his own. He used it to discover Jupiter's moons.

Today's Telescopes

People look through a telescope with just one eye. Galileo's telescope made things look 20 times closer. Today's home telescopes can make things look 100 times closer.

Parts of a Telescope

Most home telescopes have several important parts in common.

High-Powered Home Telescopes

Some people buy powerful telescopes. These devices can be expensive. But they offer advantages. They show fainter objects. Some make objects look up to 400 times closer.

Local astronomy clubs may set up powerful telescopes for visitors to use.

The company Celestron makes telescopes with large apertures.

Letting In More Light

Better telescopes have bigger apertures. An aperture is the opening that collects light. Too little light makes an image look fuzzy.

Library Resources

Many libraries hold astronomy events for beginners. These events help people get started with stargazing. People may get to use the library's telescope.

Bad weather can suddenly ruin a planned evening of stargazing.

Weather Matters

Clouds can make it hard to see objects in the night sky. Humidity can also be a problem. Humidity is the amount of moisture in the air. It can make the view fuzzy. Strong wind can make stargazing harder. It can stir up dust.

The Atmosphere

People see stars through Earth's atmosphere. Even on a clear night, the atmosphere affects stargazing. The gases can bend light from the stars.

Mountaintops are sometimes used for stargazing because they rise above part of the atmosphere.

Special Tools

People called astrophotographers take pictures of the night sky. They use special telescopes and cameras. A device called an equatorial mount is important. It keeps the telescope pointed at an object as Earth rotates.

Taking good pictures of the night sky takes patience and planning.

NASA telescopes create great images of space objects.

Images from Scientists

Some of the best images of the night sky come from scientists. They take pictures to learn about space. Many of these people work for universities. Some work for the National Aeronautics and Space Administration (NASA). This US government agency explores space.

FUN FACT!

A NASA website lets people control telescopes online. Users can choose which object to see and when to take a picture.

Holding a smartphone up to a telescope is one simple way to get pictures of the night sky.

Amateur Astronomers

Everyday people can also get great pictures of the night sky. They don't need expensive tools. People who take part in an activity for fun are called amateurs. Many amateur astronomers share their images online.

University Observatories

Some universities have very large telescopes. They are in buildings called observatories. Professors and students use them to study space. Observatories often share their images with the public.

The University of Chicago ran the Yerkes Observatory from 1897 to 2018.

Museums and Planetariums

Many science museums also have observatories. Visitors can try using their telescopes. Some museums also have planetariums. These are large rooms with domed ceilings. Projectors make the ceiling look like the night sky.

Planetarium shows are popular ways to learn about the night sky.

The Hubble Space Telescope is the size of a school bus.

Space Telescopes

NASA launches telescopes into space. These telescopes are above the atmosphere. This gives them a clearer view. The Hubble Space Telescope launched in 1990. It sends back views of stars and planets. In 2021, NASA launched the James Webb Space Telescope. It shows even more features than Hubble.

A Giant Telescope

The Gran Telescopio Canarias is one of the largest telescopes on Earth. It is in Spain's Canary Islands. It is 34 feet (10.4 m) across.

Stars are huge objects, but they are so far away they look like points of light in the night sky.

What Are Stars?

Stars are huge burning balls of gas. The sun is the closest star to Earth. The night sky is filled with more distant stars. They differ in color and size. People can see about 100,000 stars with binoculars. Telescopes let people see millions of stars.

A Lot of Zeros

Astronomers believe that there are about 200 sextillion stars in the universe. This would be a 2 followed by 23 zeros.

Moving and Changing

Stars seem to move through the sky. People can see different stars in different seasons. It is not really the stars that move, though. Earth is always rotating. It is also orbiting the sun. These movements bring different stars into view.

Photos taken over time show the movement of stars in the sky.

Rising and Setting Stars

Most stars look as though they rise in the east. This is because they become visible at the horizon. This is where the sky meets the ground. Later in the night, stars appear to set in the west. This is because of Earth's rotation. The stars aren't truly rising or setting.

Earth's rotation always affects what people see in the night sky.

Polaris is almost exactly above Earth's north pole.

Circumpolar Stars

Some stars are always visible in one hemisphere. These are called circumpolar stars. Polaris is one of them. It remains in the northern hemisphere's night sky all year. But it is never visible in the southern hemisphere.

Telescopes can bring faint stars into clearer view.

Burning Bright

Some stars look brighter than others. These stars may be larger. Or they may simply be closer. Many of the brightest stars in the night sky are both large and close to Earth.

Twinkle, Twinkle

Stars often appear to twinkle when viewed from Earth. A star's light passes through Earth's atmosphere. Moving air bends this light. This causes the twinkling.

FUN FACT!

Scientists think that most stars have planets that orbit them.

People camp in dark places to see more stars.

Brightening and Dimming

Variable stars are brighter at certain times and dimmer at others. This is because the stars are always changing in size. When they are bigger, they produce more light. As they get smaller, they produce less.

FUN FACT!

Delta Cephei was discovered to be a variable star in 1874.

Delta Cephei was the first variable star ever discovered.

Planets can be occulted too. This image shows the path of Mars moving behind the moon.

Hidden Stars

Some stars seem to vanish at times. This happens when an object such as a planet passes in front of them. This is called an occultation. The star reappears as the object moves out of the way.

Sirius is blue in color.

Sirius

Sirius is the brightest star in the night sky. If it were as distant as the sun, it would look 25 times brighter than the sun. But Sirius is very far away. Scientists measure long distances in light-years. A light-year is the distance light can travel in one year. Sirius is 8.6 light-years from Earth.

Rigel

Another bright star is Rigel. This star is 47,000 times brighter than the sun. But it is even farther away than Sirius. Rigel is 860 light-years from Earth. This great distance makes Rigel look dimmer than Sirius.

An artist's image shows what a blue supergiant like Rigel might look like from a nearby planet.

Binary Stars

Stars that orbit each other are called binary stars. They often appear as a single star to the naked eye. Stargazers can see them separately with a small telescope.

There are thousands of known binary stars.

Many Light-Years Apart

Sometimes stars in a pair do not orbit each other. They are actually far apart. People once thought a star pair called Albireo was a binary star. But scientists later learned the two stars are 380 light-years apart. They just looked close together from Earth.

CONSTELLATIONS

Imaginary lines connect stars to form constellations.

What Are Constellations?

Constellations are groups of stars. Imagining lines between the stars makes them look like people, animals, or objects. Some images are easier to see than others. Drawing a map of the stars and connecting them like dots can make a constellation clearer.

FUN FACT!

There are a total of 88 officially recognized constellations.

The Pictures of Mythology

Ancient people created myths to explain how nature worked. Many myths came from ancient Greece. Constellations represent their gods, heroes, and creatures. Even today, constellations remind people of these ancient stories.

The night-sky traditions of ancient Greece are still around today.

Farther Apart Than They Look

Dubhe and Megrez appear next to each other in Ursa Major. But they are actually about 42 light-years apart.

Ursa Major

Ursa Major is the largest northern constellation. It never sets below the horizon. But it does appear low in the sky during winter. Its brightest star is Alioth. This white star is also part of a star pattern called the Big Dipper.

The Big Dipper forms Ursa Major's rear end and tail.

An illustration from the 1830s shows Ursa Major and its stars.

The Great Bear

Ursa Major means "greater bear" in Latin. The constellation is linked to the Greek myth of Callisto. The god Zeus fell in love with Callisto. But Zeus was already married to the goddess Hera. Hera became jealous. In some tellings of the story, she turned Callisto into a bear.

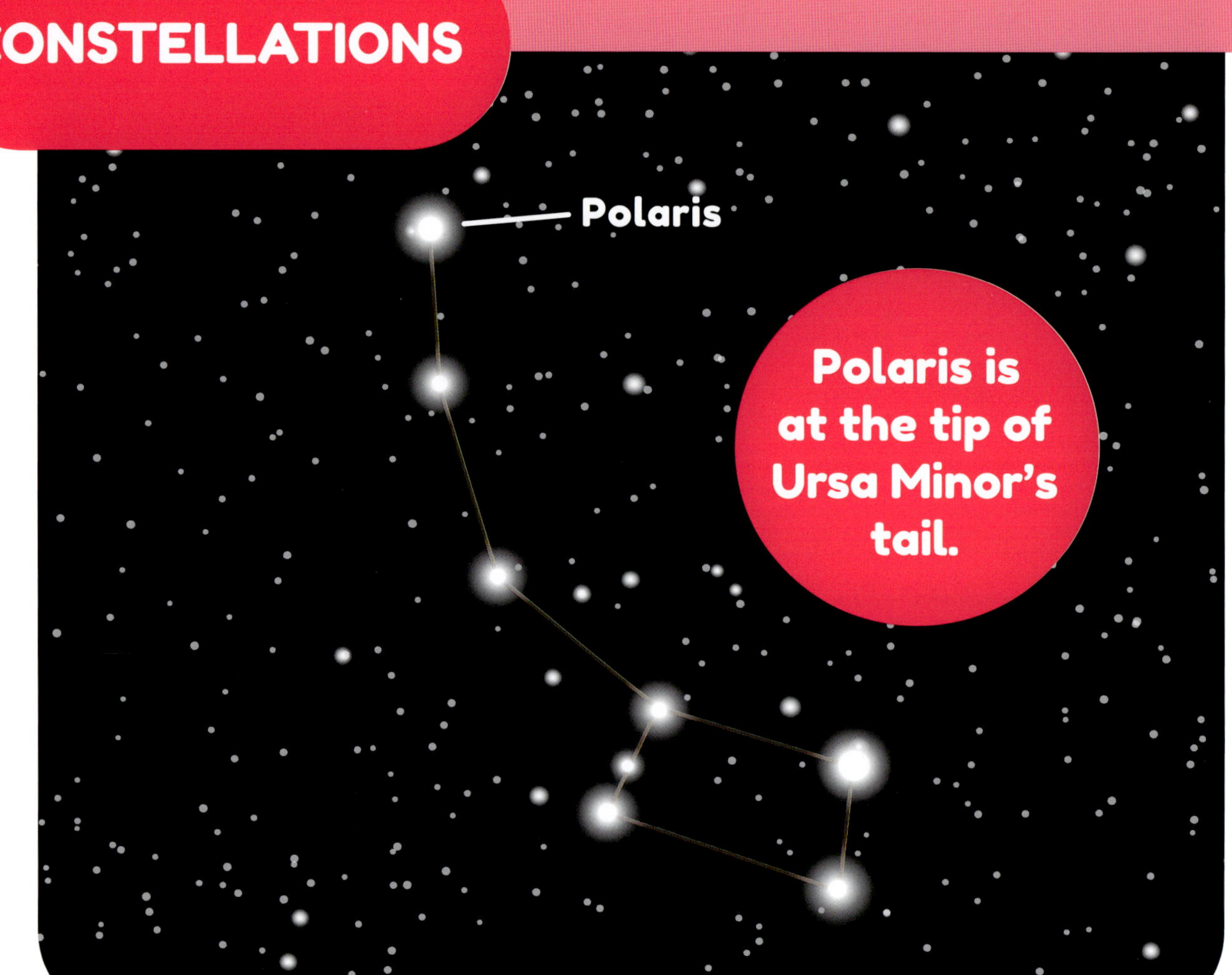

Ursa Minor

Like Ursa Major, Ursa Minor never leaves the northern sky. Its brightest star is Polaris. This variable star changes in brightness about every four days. Ursa Minor also has a star pattern called the Little Dipper.

The Little Bear

Ursa Minor means "smaller bear" in Latin. In a Greek myth, Ursa Minor represents Arcas. He is the son of Zeus and Callisto. In one telling of the story, Zeus turned both Callisto and Arcas into bears. He did this to protect them from Hera.

Arcas is a hunter in Greek mythology.

Just Getting Started

Betelgeuse is young compared with many other stars. Earth's sun is almost 5 billion years old. Betelgeuse has existed for only about 10 million years.

Orion

Orion is one of the best-known constellations. People can see it in both hemispheres. More than a dozen stars make up Orion. The two brightest are Betelgeuse and Rigel. Betelgeuse is a red supergiant. It is Orion's right shoulder. Rigel is a blue supergiant. It is Orion's left foot.

The three stars close together in Orion are known as Orion's Belt.

Drawings of the Orion constellation sometimes show him holding a club and a lion.

The Hunter's Story

In Greek mythology, Orion was a powerful hunter. But he died from a scorpion sting. The gods then placed both the hunter and the scorpion in the sky. The scorpion became the constellation Scorpius. These two constellations are never visible at the same time.

FUN FACT!

Betelgeuse is almost 1,000 times bigger than the sun.

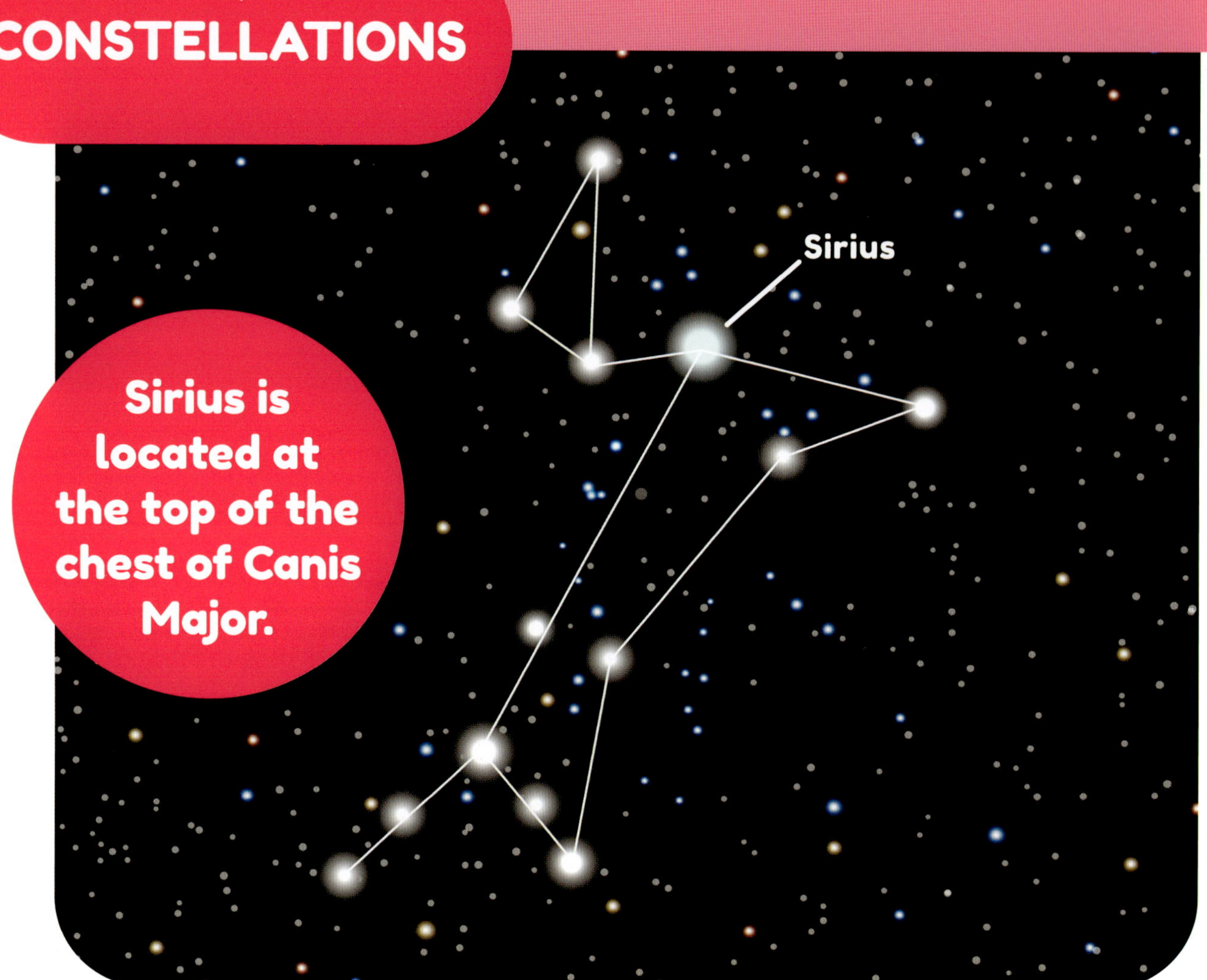

Canis Major and Canis Minor

People can see Canis Major and Canis Minor in both hemispheres. *Canis Major* means "greater dog" in Latin. *Canis Minor* means "smaller dog." Canis Major's brightest star is Sirius. The brightest star in Canis Minor is Procyon.

Orion's Dogs

In Greek myths, Canis Major and Canis Minor were Orion's hunting dogs. In the sky, the larger dog appears to be chasing a nearby constellation of a hare. One story said Zeus turned both dogs into stone before putting them in the sky.

Canis Minor is a small constellation with just two main stars.

Cassiopeia

Cassiopeia's simple shape makes the constellation easy to spot. The constellation looks like the letter *W* when it is high in the sky. When it is lower, it looks like the letter *M*. There are even times when it looks like a zigzag.

Cassiopeia has been recognized as a constellation for almost 2,000 years.

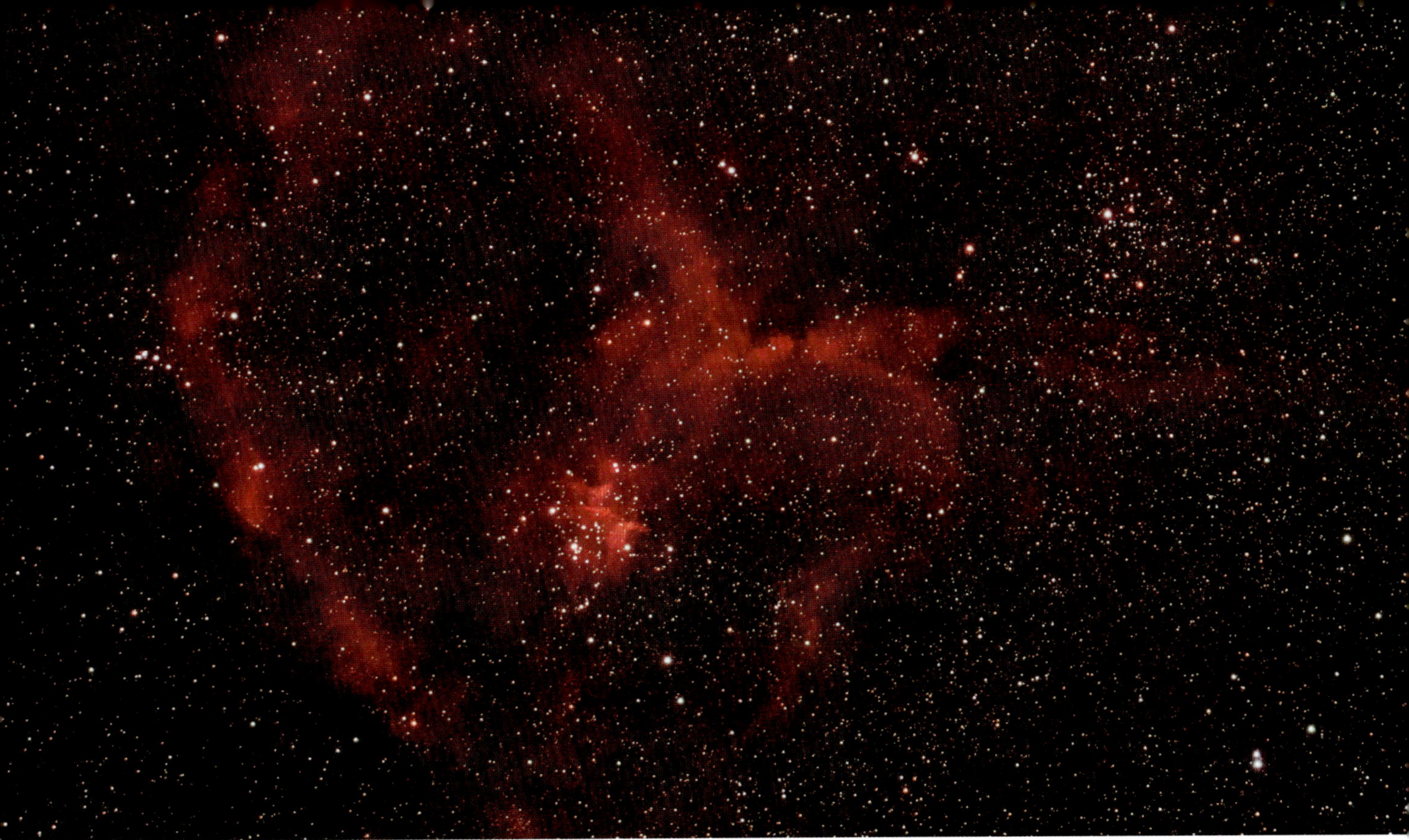

Powerful telescopes reveal colorful nebulae inside the Cassiopeia constellation.

The Queen

Cassiopeia was a queen in Greek mythology. She angered the sea god Poseidon by claiming she was more beautiful than his wife. Poseidon sent a sea monster to her kingdom. She escaped the monster. But Poseidon still punished the queen. He put her in the stars and made her circle the night sky forever.

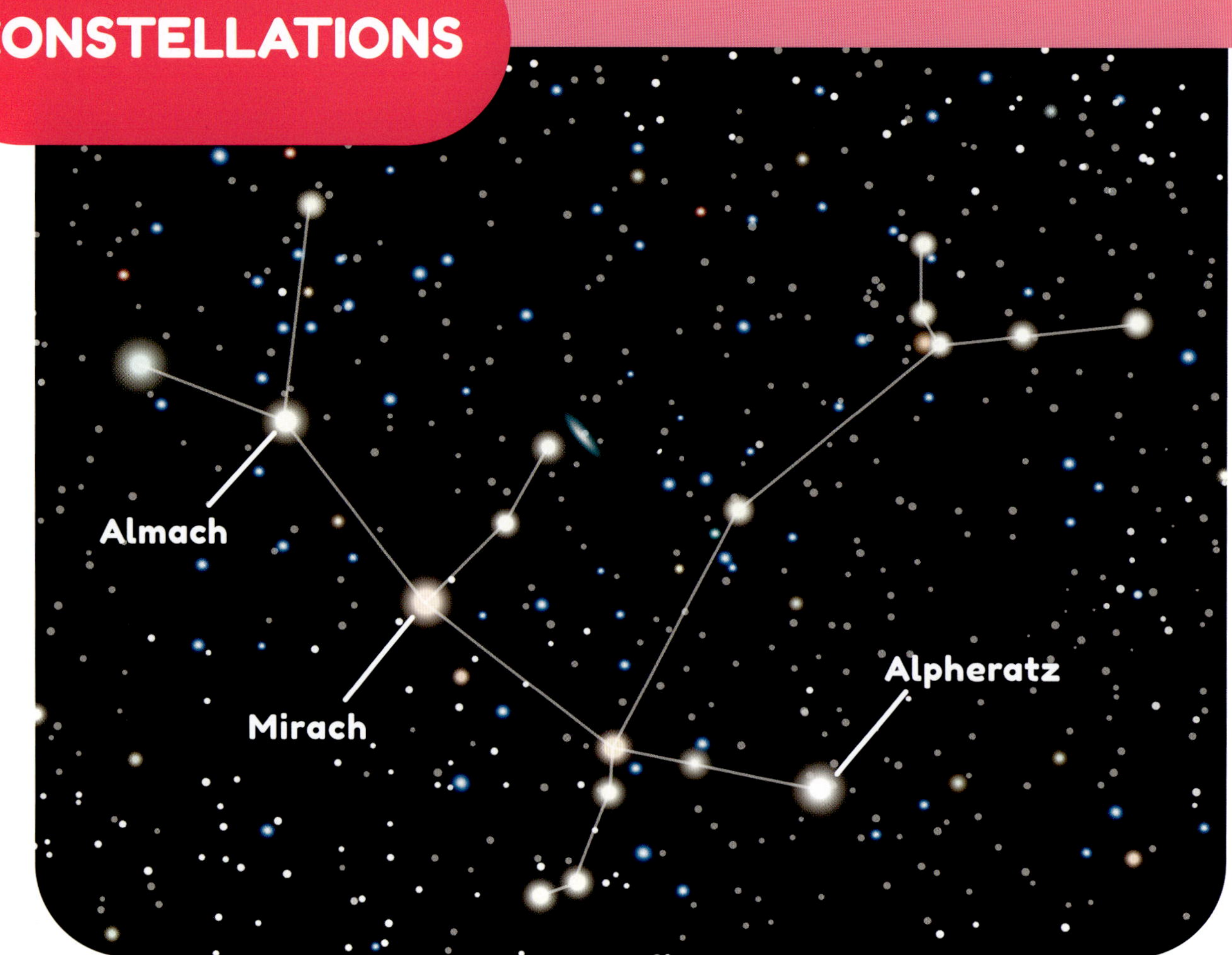

The brightest stars in Andromeda are Alpheratz, Mirach, and Almach.

Andromeda

The constellation Andromeda represents a princess chained to a rock. Andromeda appears in the northern night sky. It is best seen in fall and winter.

The Chained Princess

In Greek myths, Andromeda was the daughter of Cassiopeia and Cepheus. When Poseidon's sea monster attacked, the parents left Andromeda chained to a rock. They were trying to save themselves and their kingdom. It looked as if the monster would kill the princess. But the hero Perseus saved her.

The stories of Andromeda and Perseus are closely linked.

Perseus

Perseus is next to Andromeda in the northern sky. Its brightest star is Mirfak. But its best-known star is Algol. It is a binary star. When viewed from Earth, one star sometimes passes in front of the other. This makes Algol's brightness change over time.

The California Nebula is located within Perseus.

The Hero Who Saved the Day

The hero Perseus played a key part in the Andromeda myth. He came across the princess by chance. He saved her before the monster found her. Andromeda then married Perseus. The gods made Perseus and Andromeda into constellations to honor them.

Actor Sam Worthington played Perseus in the 2010 movie *Clash of the Titans.*

Pegasus is most easily seen in autumn in the northern hemisphere.

Pegasus

Pegasus is a large constellation. It represents a winged horse from Greek mythology. The constellation includes a star pattern called the Great Square. This pattern forms the body of the horse.

The Winged Horse

In Greek mythology, there was a fierce creature called the Chimera. No one was able to defeat the Chimera because it breathed fire. But the hero Bellerophon tamed Pegasus. Together they attacked the Chimera. They killed the creature.

There is a statue in Turkey of Pegasus and Bellerophon battling the Chimera.

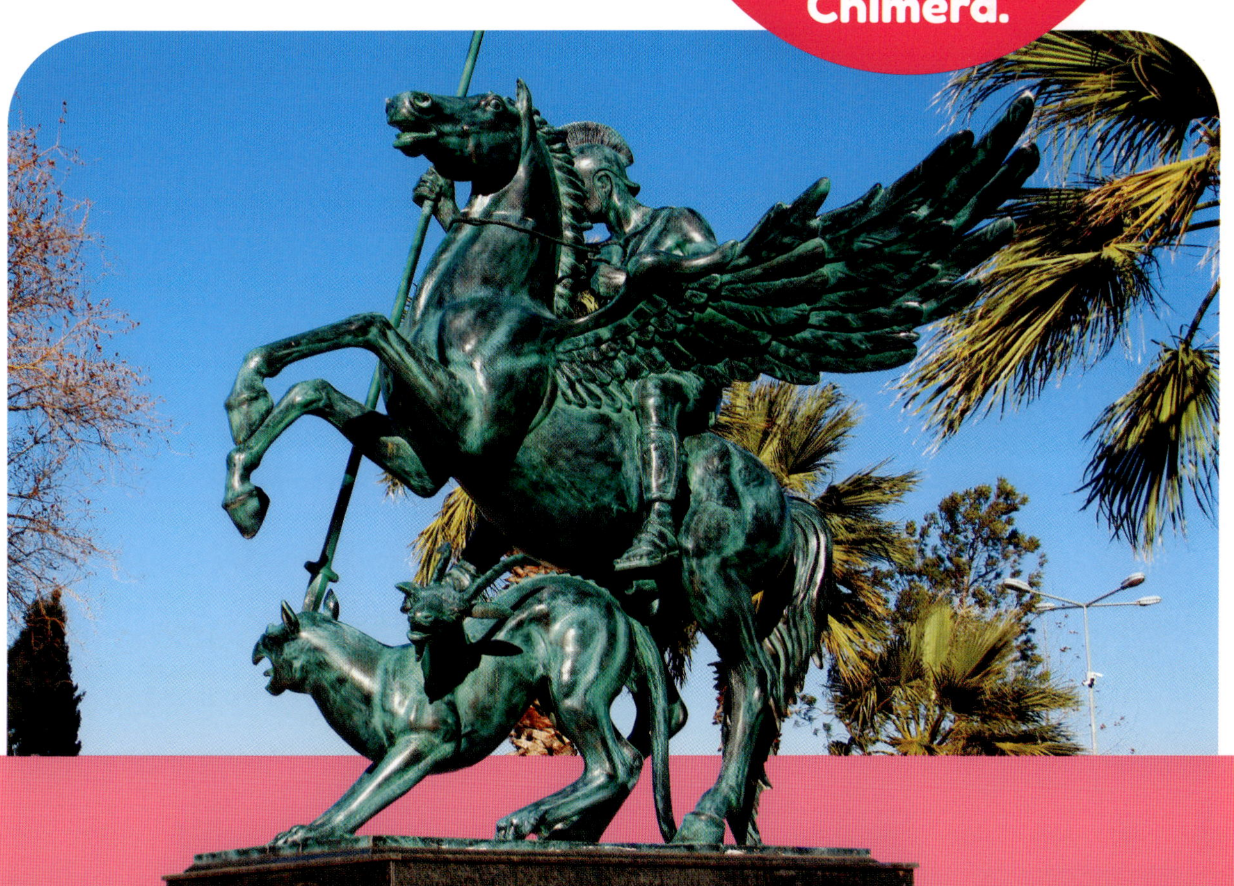

Draco

The northern constellation Draco represents a dragon. Eltanin is Draco's brightest star. It forms the dragon's eye.

Many stars form Draco's long, twisting body in the night sky.

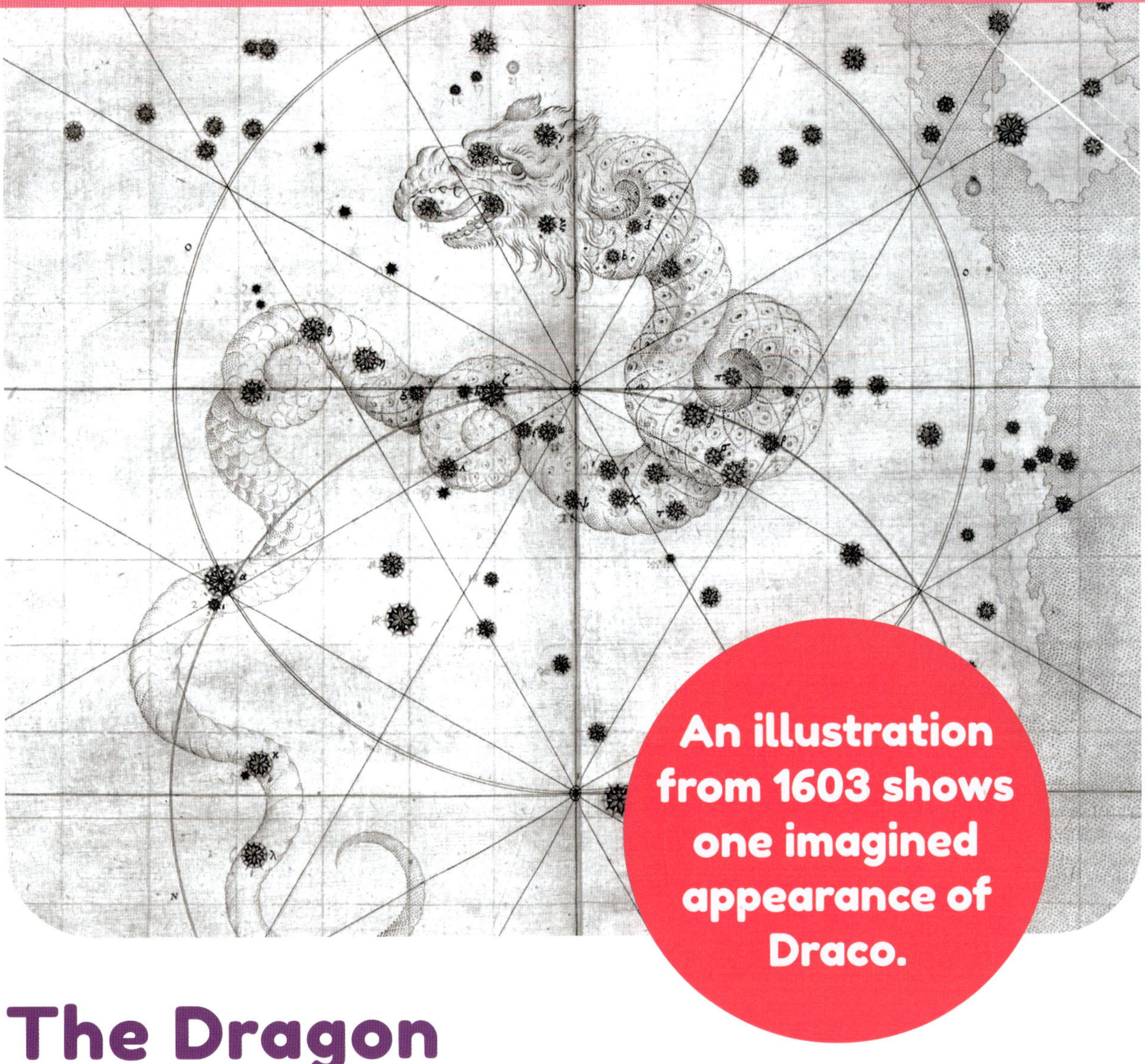

An illustration from 1603 shows one imagined appearance of Draco.

The Dragon

Draco appeared in a Greek myth about Hera. The queen received a golden apple tree as a wedding gift. She placed a dragon near the tree to guard it. But the hero Heracles stole the apples. He killed the dragon with poisoned arrows.

The two horns sticking out, *left*, are important parts of Taurus.

Taurus the Bull

Many people find Taurus in the night sky by first finding Orion. The hunter's belt includes three stars. They form a line that helps stargazers find Aldebaran. This orange-red star makes up the eye of Taurus the bull. This constellation represents the zodiac sign of the same name.

The Zodiac Constellations

The ancient Mesopotamians believed stars guided human life. They divided the night sky into 12 sections. Within each one is a constellation. The sun moves through all these sections over the course of a year. A person's zodiac sign is based on where the sun is in the sky when they are born.

Ancient astronomy combined observations of the night sky with beliefs about fate.

Leo the Lion

Leo is one of the easiest zodiac constellations to spot. This constellation represents a lion. Six stars form its head. They look like a backward question mark. Three more stars form the lion's rear. Leo's brightest star is Regulus.

The fight between Heracles and the lion is often shown in art.

Wrestling a Lion

Greek mythology includes stories linked to the zodiac constellations. In one myth, Heracles must kill a lion. But no weapons can pierce the animal's hide. The hero succeeds by wrestling the lion. Hera rewards the lion's bravery by placing it among the stars.

Different people imagine the picture around a constellation in a wide variety of ways.

Sagittarius the Archer

Sagittarius is an archer. But some people see different things within the constellation. Some see a centaur holding a bow and arrow. A centaur is half human and half horse. Others see just an arrow and a bow. The brightest star in Sagittarius is Kaus Australis.

Many Myths

The Mesopotamians linked this constellation to their war god Nergal. The Greeks often linked Sagittarius to Chiron the centaur. The wise Chiron taught heroes in Greek mythology.

Stories sometimes include centaurs using bows and arrows.

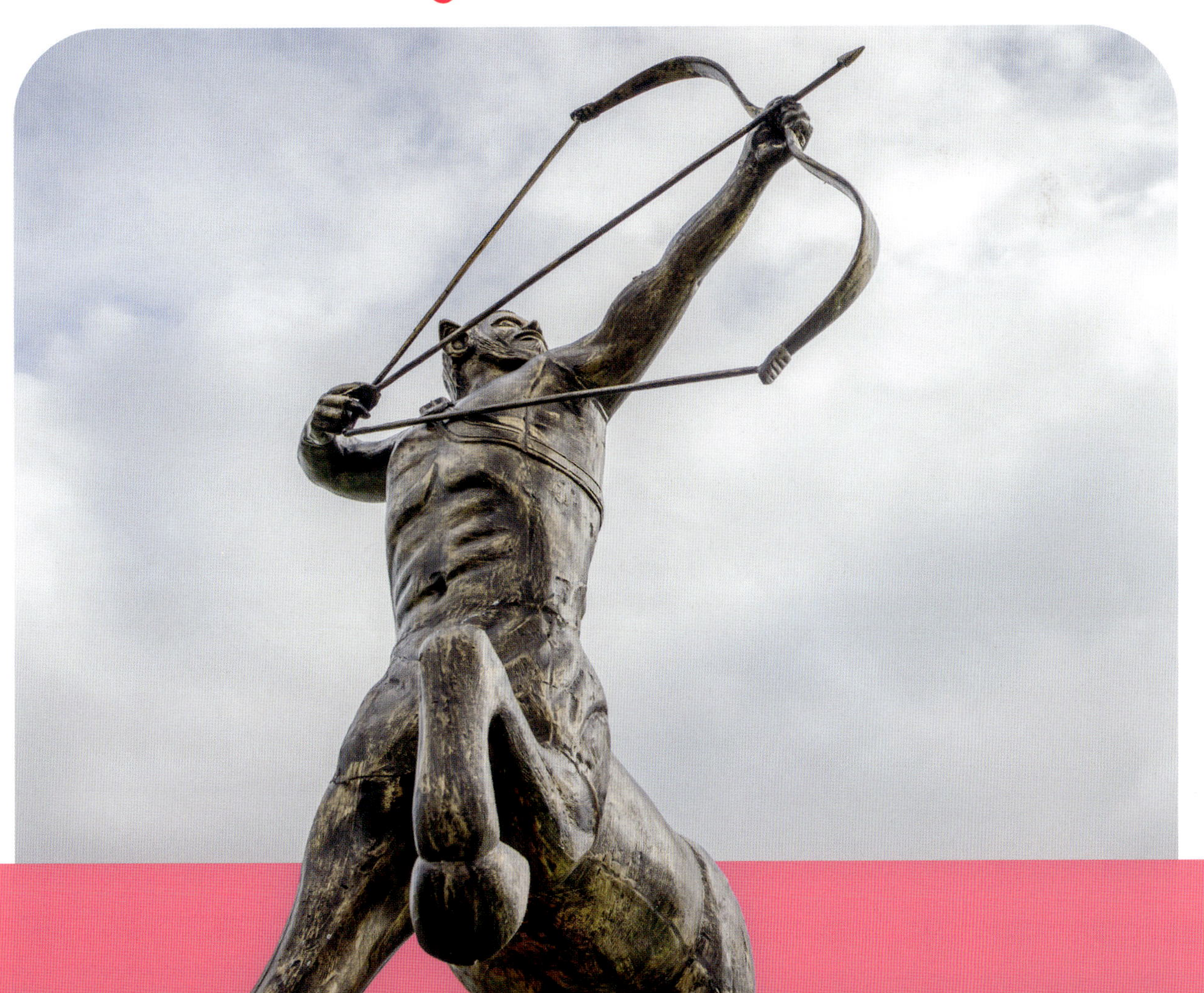

What Are Planets?

Planets are celestial bodies that orbit a star. Besides Earth, there are seven planets in the solar system. They are much closer to Earth than the stars. People can see Mercury, Venus, Mars, Jupiter, and Saturn with the naked eye. Uranus can be seen faintly. Seeing Neptune requires a telescope.

In the night sky, nearby planets look smaller than the moon but larger than stars.

The solar system's planets are popular viewing targets for stargazers.

Spotting Planets

Unlike stars, planets do not twinkle. But a planet's brightness changes over time. Planets reflect sunlight. A planet looks brighter when it is closer to Earth. It may also appear brighter when it is higher in the sky.

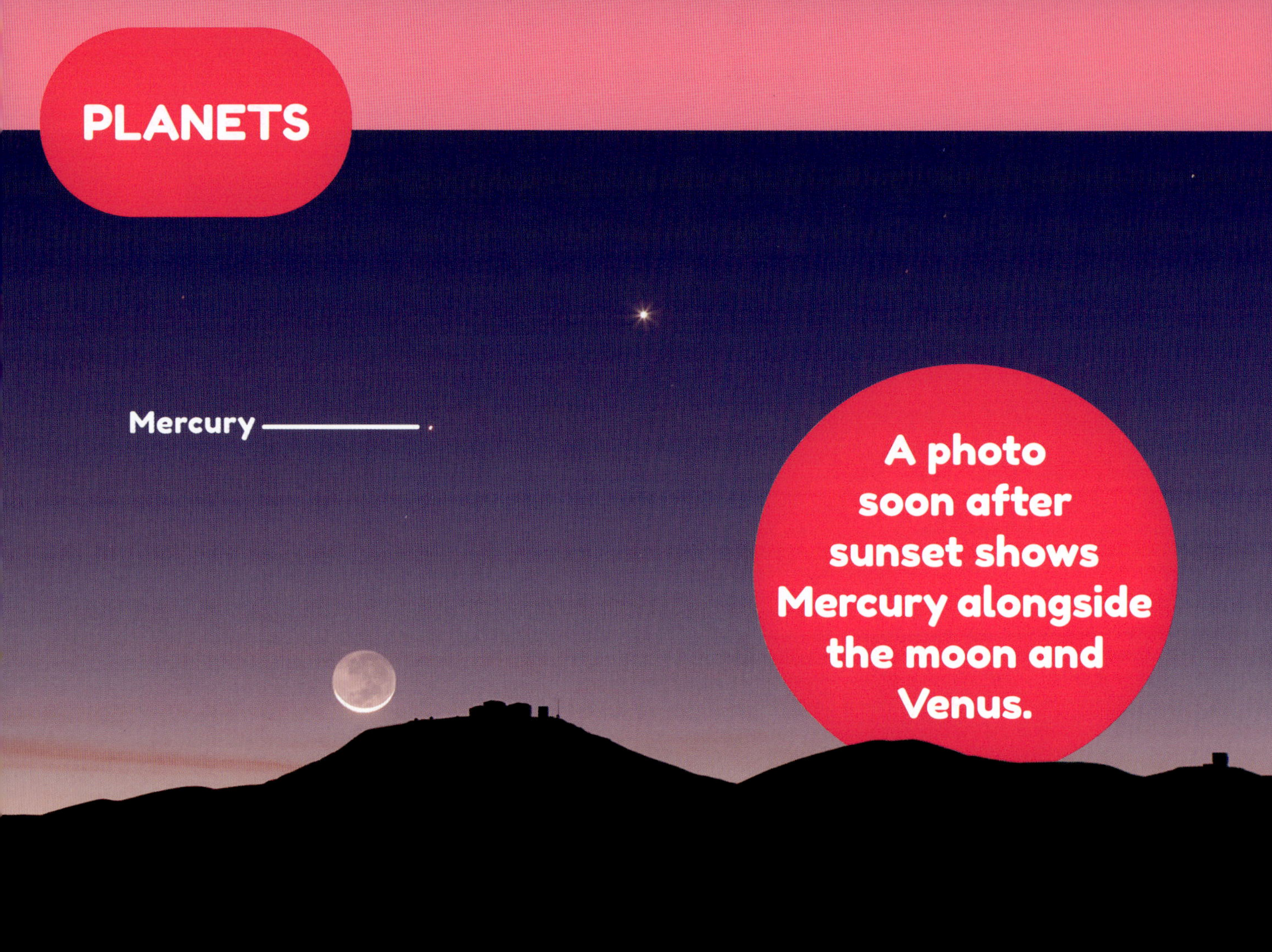

A photo soon after sunset shows Mercury alongside the moon and Venus.

Mercury

Stargazers can see Mercury from Earth. But spotting it is tricky. This is because Mercury is the closest planet to the sun. The sun's brightness usually outshines it. The best times for viewing Mercury are dawn and twilight.

The Phases of Mercury

Mercury goes through phases much like Earth's moon. The planet may appear as a crescent shape or a half-disk. People cannot see the planet when it is fully lit. Mercury is behind the sun at this time.

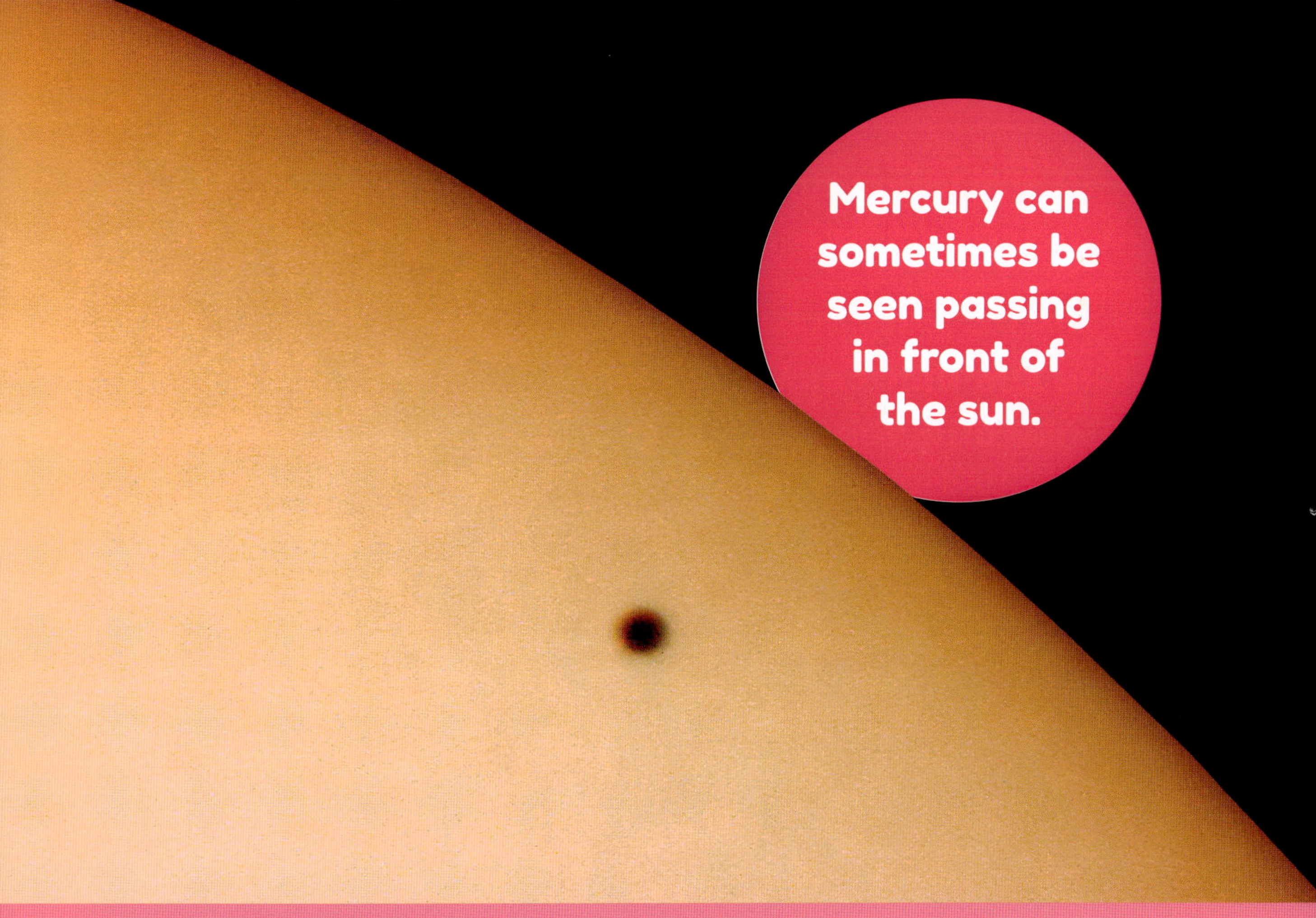

Venus

Venus is the brightest planet in the night sky. This is partly because it is so close to Earth. Another reason is that Venus is covered with thick clouds. They reflect the sun's light.

Venus is the second-brightest object in the night sky behind the moon.

Venus

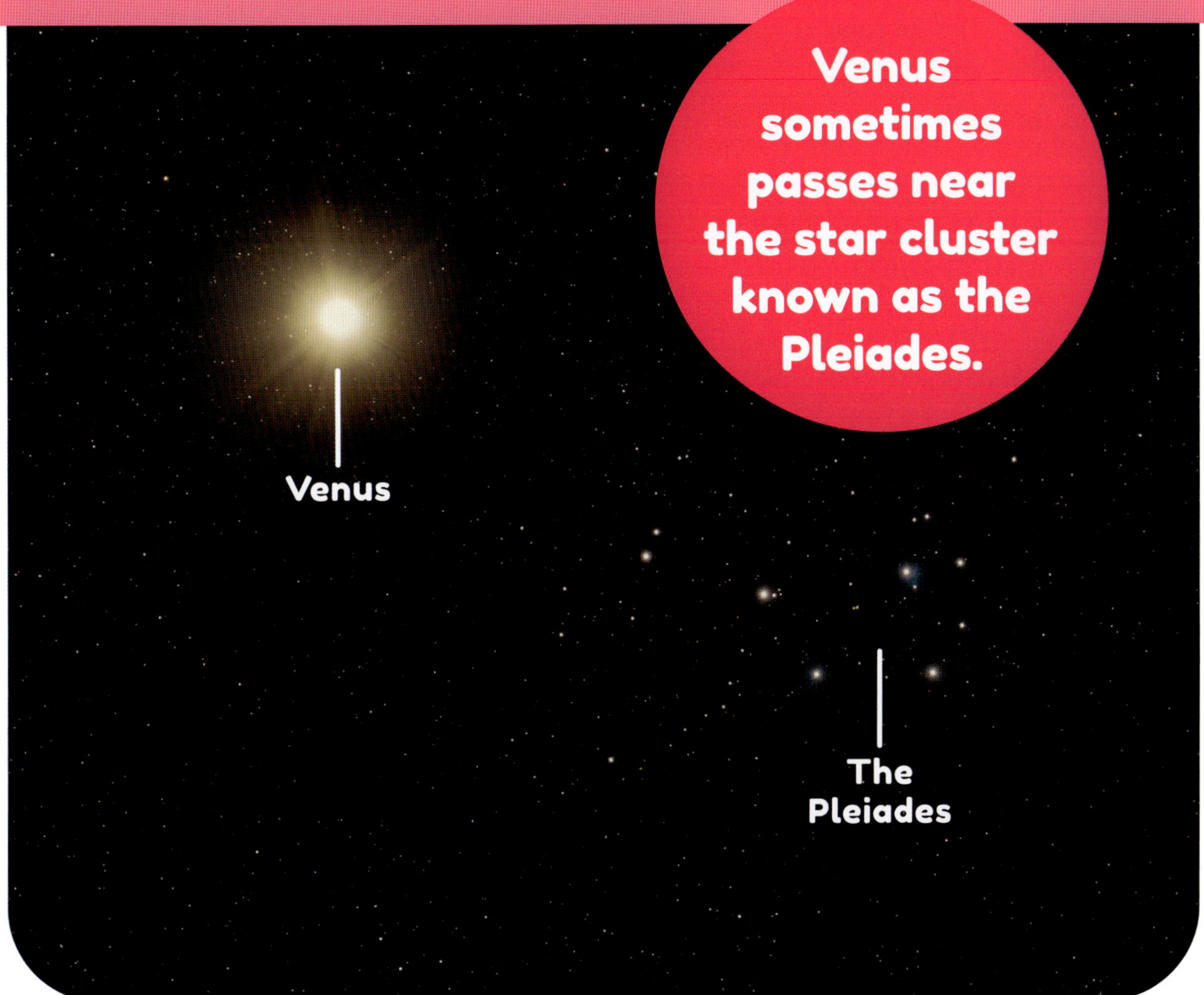

Best Viewing Times

Stargazers can see Venus before sunrise or after sunset. It is visible in the morning for about 263 days. Then it is visible in the evening for 263 days. People have called Venus both the morning star and the evening star.

Mars is nicknamed the Red Planet.

Mars

The surface of Mars is colored brown, gold, and tan. But the planet looks red from Earth. Many of the rocks on Mars have iron. Wind blows this element into the planet's atmosphere. It gives the planet its famous red appearance.

Moving Closer

Planets orbit the sun in an oval pattern. They also get closer or farther away from Earth as they move. When they are closer, planets appear bigger and brighter. Mars reaches its closest point about every two years.

Earth's best telescopes can take stunning pictures of Mars.

Jupiter

Jupiter is the largest planet. This makes it easy to spot from Earth. Its closest point to Earth comes every 13 months. To the naked eye, it looks like a yellow-white dot in the night sky.

FUN FACT!

Although they are far apart, Mars and Jupiter sometimes look like they are almost touching.

Jupiter appears as the brightest night-sky object in this image.

People can use backyard telescopes to see Jupiter's clouds and its largest moons.

Great Red Spot and Moons

People with telescopes can see many more features. They can observe Jupiter's Great Red Spot. This is a huge storm. Binoculars or telescopes reveal Jupiter's four largest moons. One of them, Ganymede, is the biggest moon in the solar system.

Numbers Vary

Some planets have multiple moons. Others have none. Earth has just one moon.

Saturn and Jupiter sometimes appear side by side in the night sky. This is called a conjunction.

Saturn

Saturn is easy to see with the naked eye. It looks like a yellow dot. But stargazers can see something special with binoculars or a telescope. This planet has rings around it. Jupiter, Uranus, and Neptune also have rings. But Saturn's rings are the largest and brightest.

Disappearing Act

Saturn is tilted. Earth's view of the planet changes over time. Sometimes the rings are lined up with Earth. Only the edges are seen. The rings become hard to see. Other times Saturn's tilt makes the rings look clear and bright.

Astronomer Christiaan Huygens observed and drew Saturn's rings in the 1600s.

Uranus

Uranus was the first planet astronomers discovered using a telescope. Uranus is four times wider than Earth. But it is also very far away. For this reason, people can't see many features from Earth. Uranus looks like a small green dot even through a large telescope.

FUN FACT!

The distance between the planets is always changing. This is because they orbit the sun at different distances.

A powerful telescope in Chile captured this image of Uranus.

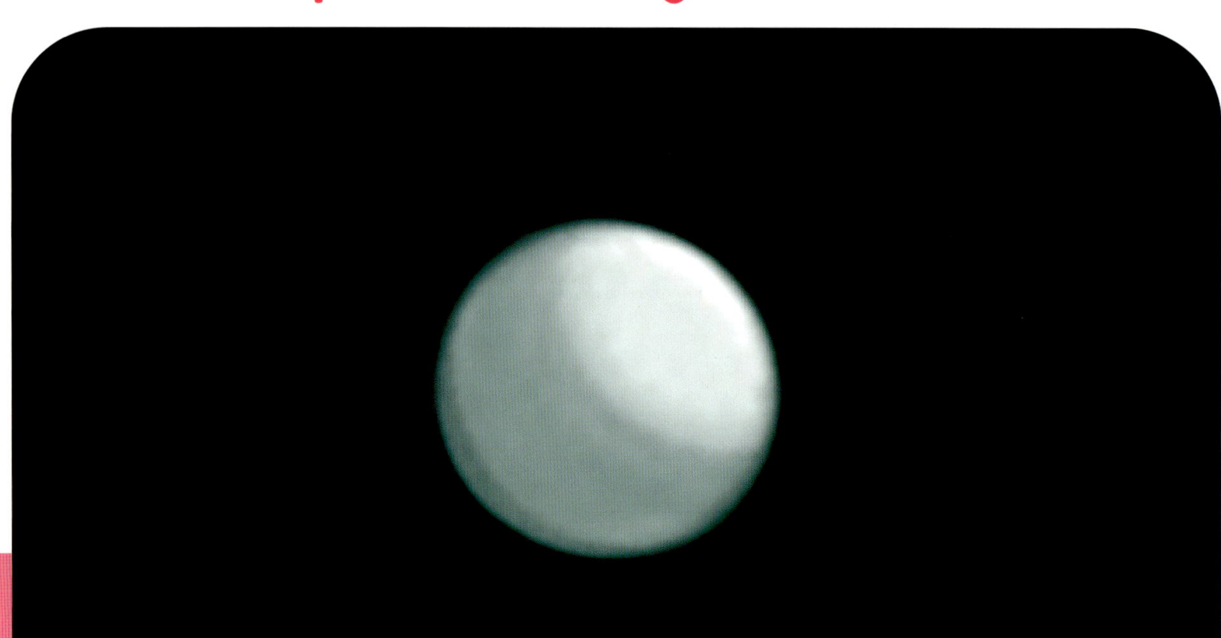

Earth's largest telescopes can observe the rings of Uranus.

Spinning Sideways

Uranus is very tilted. Scientists think a large object may have crashed into it in the past. This may have caused the tilt. The planet's tilt makes Uranus look as if it is rotating sideways.

Getting good images of Neptune required sending a spacecraft to the distant planet.

Neptune

Neptune is the farthest planet from the sun. People can see it with a small telescope. But they can't see its features. Neptune is 30 times farther from the sun than Earth is. The planet appears very dim. It looks like a small blue-green speck.

Seeing Triton

Neptune has 16 known moons. The largest is Triton. People with powerful telescopes can see both Neptune and Triton.

Neptune and Triton are visible at the center of this telescope image. They can be hard to pick out from background stars.

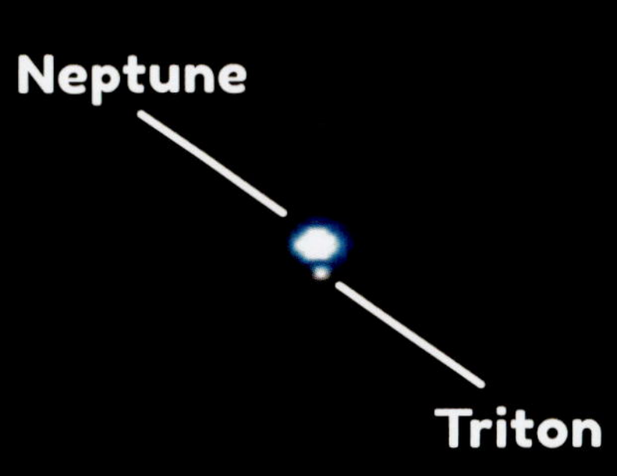

What Is the Moon?

A satellite is an object in space that orbits another object. Natural satellites are also called moons. Earth's natural satellite is simply known as the moon.

FUN FACT!

The moon is slowly moving away from Earth. Each year, it gets about 1.5 inches (3.8 cm) farther away.

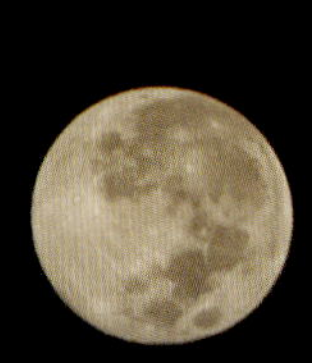

The moon is the nearest large space object to Earth.

Unlike many stars, the moon is visible even with bright city lights nearby.

Why Does the Moon Shine?

The moon appears in the sky almost every night when the weather is clear. It is the brightest object in the night sky. But it does not give off its own light. The moon reflects light from the sun.

The Dark Side of the Moon

The same side of the moon always faces Earth. Some people call the other side the moon's dark side. But this nickname is not correct. The far side receives just as much sunlight as the near side.

Telescopes reveal a lot of features on the moon's surface.

The Moon's Surface

The moon's rocky surface is easy to see from Earth. It has both light and dark areas. The light areas are called highlands. The dark areas are called maria. The moon is also covered with many craters.

Shapes in the Moon

Many people see shapes in the moon's surface. One of the most common is a man's face. People often call this the man in the moon. Other shapes that people see include a rabbit and a toad.

A rabbit is closely linked with the moon in Chinese culture.

Changing Shapes

The moon goes through eight phases. This takes 29.5 days. In the new moon phase, the sun lights the moon's far side. The moon looks dark from Earth. Gradually more of the moon lights up. Finally it is fully lit up. This is the full moon phase.

A full moon gives stargazers the most complete view of its surface.

The moon becomes a slim crescent as more of its lit-up side faces away from Earth.

Waxing and Waning

As more of the moon lights up, people say it is waxing. After the full moon, it begins waning. Less of the satellite becomes visible. The moon appears as a waning crescent just before reaching the new moon phase.

A supermoon rises over a mountain in Italy.

Supermoons

The moon orbits Earth in an oval shape. It moves closer or farther from Earth. A supermoon happens when the moon is closest to Earth and full at the same time. It looks especially big and bright. Supermoons happen three or four times each year.

Micromoons

The moon also looks smaller at certain times. A micromoon happens when the moon is farthest from Earth and full at the same time. It looks less bright than normal. Micromoons happen two or three times each year.

The moon at its farthest, *left*, looks noticeably smaller than the moon at its closest, *right*.

Lunar Eclipses

Earth sometimes moves between the moon and the sun. Earth's shadow is cast on the moon. This event is called a lunar eclipse. People can see lunar eclipses from Earth with the naked eye. But many people also like to view them with telescopes.

There are usually about two lunar eclipses each year.

This photo of a lunar eclipse shows the moon's red color.

When the Moon Turns Red

The moon turns red during a lunar eclipse. Some sunlight still reaches the moon. It travels through Earth's atmosphere. The gases make the light look red.

FUN FACT!

When the moon looks red during a lunar eclipse, it is sometimes called a blood moon.

This combined image shows how the moon's color changes as it gets near the horizon.

An Orange Moon

The moon often looks orange when it is near the horizon. The moon's reflected light passes through more of Earth's atmosphere. The gases bend the light to make it appear orange.

A Blue Moon

It is rare for the moon to appear blue. But this does happen sometimes. Dust in Earth's atmosphere causes this. Ash from volcanoes can make this happen. Smoke from wildfires can cause it too.

Colorful Names

Sometimes two full moons happen within one month. The second one is called a blue moon. When this happens with two new moons, the second is called a black moon.

Materials in the atmosphere can shade the moon blue or other colors.

The Moon Illusion

The moon looks bigger to the human eye when it is near the horizon. However, it is really the same size. This is called the moon illusion. Scientists aren't sure why this illusion happens.

Seeing the moon near objects on Earth, such as trees, can make it look larger.

Camera tricks can make the moon look far larger than it really is.

Photography Tricks

Pictures of a large moon near the horizon exist. But photographers use special tricks to make the moon look bigger. They use a long camera lens. Then they use a zoomed-in view.

Telescopes reveal the colors and shapes of distant galaxies.

What Is a Galaxy?

A galaxy is a large group of stars. Gravity holds them together. A single galaxy can have billions of stars. There may be more than 100 billion galaxies in the universe.

FUN FACT!

The amount of time it takes a galaxy to orbit around its center is called a galactic year.

Types of Galaxies

There are four basic types of galaxies. Spiral galaxies are the most common. They look like giant pinwheels. Elliptical galaxies are oval in shape. Lenticular galaxies are a cross between the spiral and elliptical types. There are also irregular galaxies. They have varying shapes.

The Milky Way

Earth is in the Milky Way galaxy. This spiral galaxy has several hundred billion stars. People can see parts of the Milky Way. It looks like a band of light in the night sky. Interstellar dust makes it hard to see some other parts of it.

Light Pollution

About 80 percent of people in North America cannot see the Milky Way. This is because of all the electric lights that humans use. Stargazers call this light pollution.

Talented astrophotographers can take grand photos of the Milky Way.

Scientists have created images of what they think the Milky Way galaxy looks like.

Outstretched Arms

All spiral galaxies have arms. The arms wind around the center. Scientists once thought the Milky Way had four arms. But scientists now think it has just two.

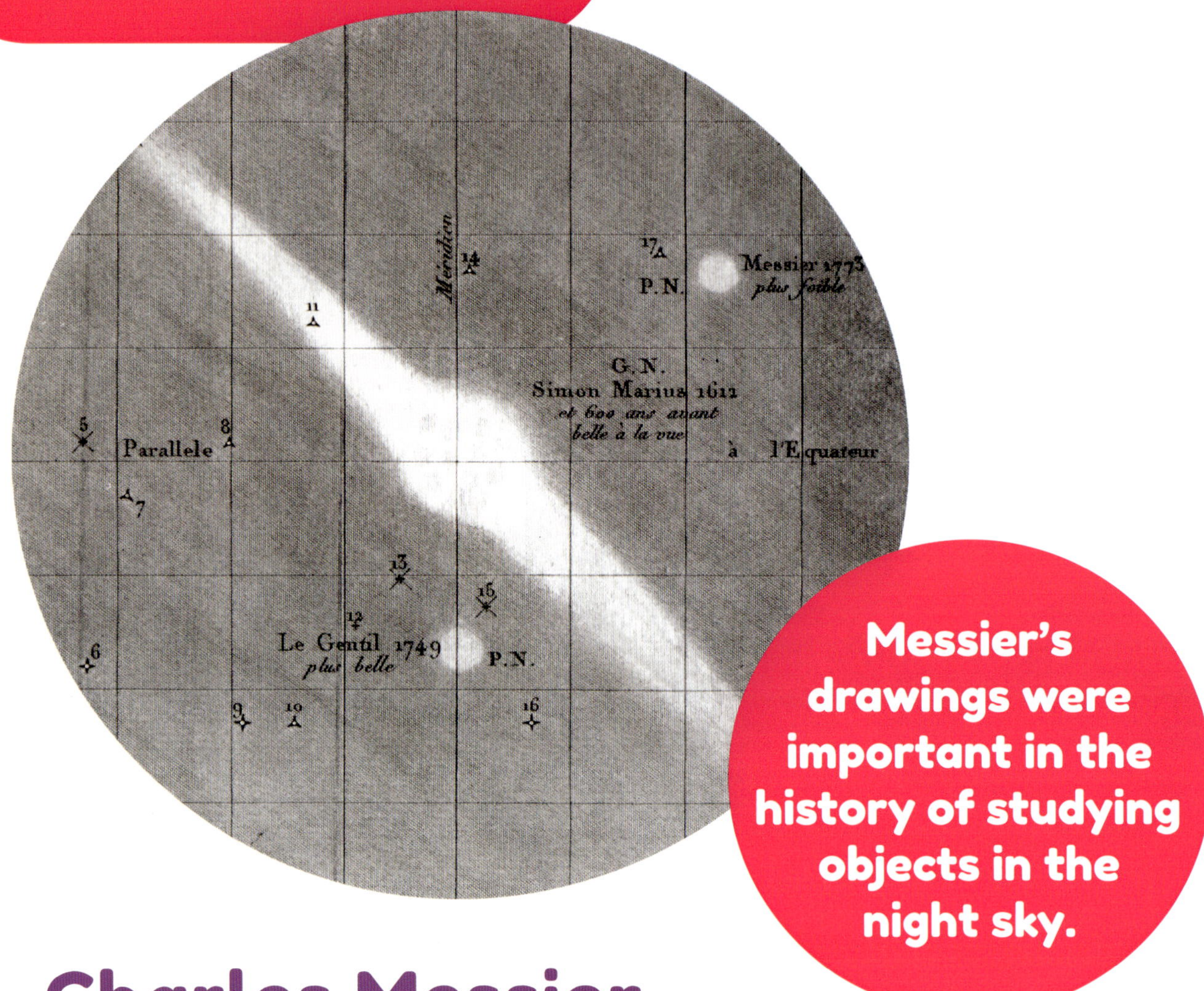

Messier's drawings were important in the history of studying objects in the night sky.

Charles Messier

In the 1700s, French astronomer Charles Messier studied the sky. He looked at objects other than individual stars or planets. These included galaxies, clusters of stars, and more. He published a numbered list of these objects.

Messier Numbers

Messier's list included 103 objects. Seven more were added later. This list is still used today. Astronomers identify objects by the numbers in the list. They use the letter *M* and a number. For example, M51 is the Whirlpool galaxy.

The Whirlpool galaxy, *right*, is next to a smaller galaxy.

Andromeda Galaxy

The closest galaxy to the Milky Way is Andromeda. It is also known as M31. It is a spiral galaxy. People can sometimes see Andromeda with the naked eye. It is the only galaxy visible without binoculars or a telescope.

The Andromeda galaxy rises in the sky over a mountain range.

Learning Experience

Observing the Andromeda galaxy helps scientists understand the Milky Way better. It is difficult to learn about a galaxy when one is inside it. NASA compares this to trying to learn the layout of New York City while standing in Central Park.

The Large Magellanic Cloud, *top right*, and the Small Magellanic Cloud, *middle right*, are near the Milky Way in the sky.

Large Magellanic Cloud

The Large Magellanic Cloud (LMC) is an irregular dwarf galaxy. It orbits the Milky Way. Dwarf galaxies are smaller than regular ones. People in the southern hemisphere can see the LMC even without a telescope. Its 30 billion stars look like fuzzy clouds.

Small Magellanic Cloud

The Small Magellanic Cloud (SMC) is even smaller. This irregular dwarf galaxy has only 3 billion stars. It is also visible to the naked eye. Scientists named the LMC and the SMC after explorer Ferdinand Magellan. His crew saw them during a sea voyage in the 1500s.

Telescopes help people see the many stars in the SMC.

M110

M110 is an elliptical dwarf galaxy. It orbits the Andromeda galaxy. People can see M110 with a small telescope. It looks like a faint patch of light. More powerful telescopes reveal an oval shape with a bright center.

Charles Messier discovered M110.

A bright spot of light near the Andromeda galaxy is M32.

M32

M32 is a smaller satellite of the Andromeda galaxy. This elliptical dwarf galaxy is best seen from the northern hemisphere in November. It looks like a spot of light with a small telescope. More powerful telescopes show clearer features.

Nebulae are often named for their appearance. This image shows the Dumbbell Nebula, or M27.

What Are Nebulae?

Nebulae are giant clouds of gas and dust in space. They are often called star nurseries. This is because stars form in them. NASA's space telescopes have captured many stunning images of nebulae.

Types of Nebulae

Many types of nebulae exist. Emission nebulae give off their own light. Reflection nebulae reflect the light of nearby stars. Dark nebulae give off no light. They look like dark smudges.

FUN FACT!

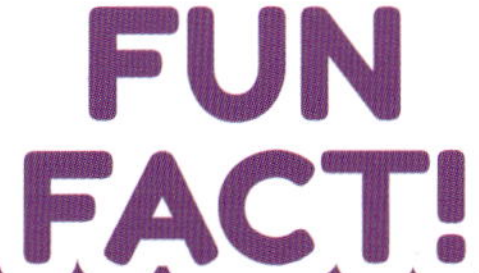

Dark nebulae block the view of objects behind them.

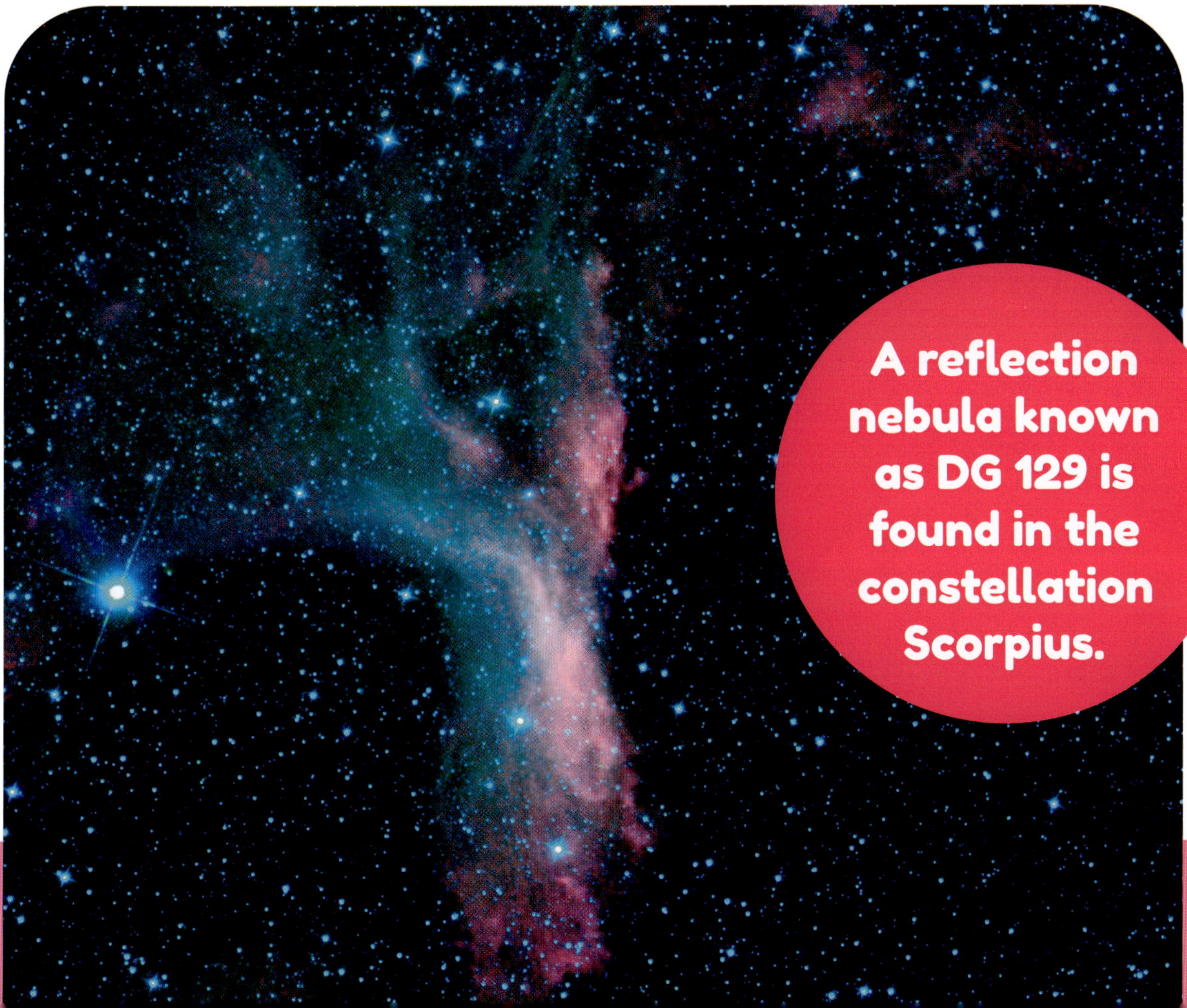

A reflection nebula known as DG 129 is found in the constellation Scorpius.

Orion Nebula

The Orion Nebula is also known as M42. It is an emission nebula. Stargazers can see it with the naked eye. People can find it by locating the Orion constellation. The nebula is halfway down the hunter's sword. It looks like a fuzzy star.

The Orion Nebula is one of the brightest nebulae in the night sky.

A star explosion created the Crab Nebula in the year 1054.

Crab Nebula

The Crab Nebula got its name because early drawings of it looked like the animal. It is also called M1. People can most easily find this nebula in January. It forms a triangle with two stars. These are Betelgeuse and Aldebaran.

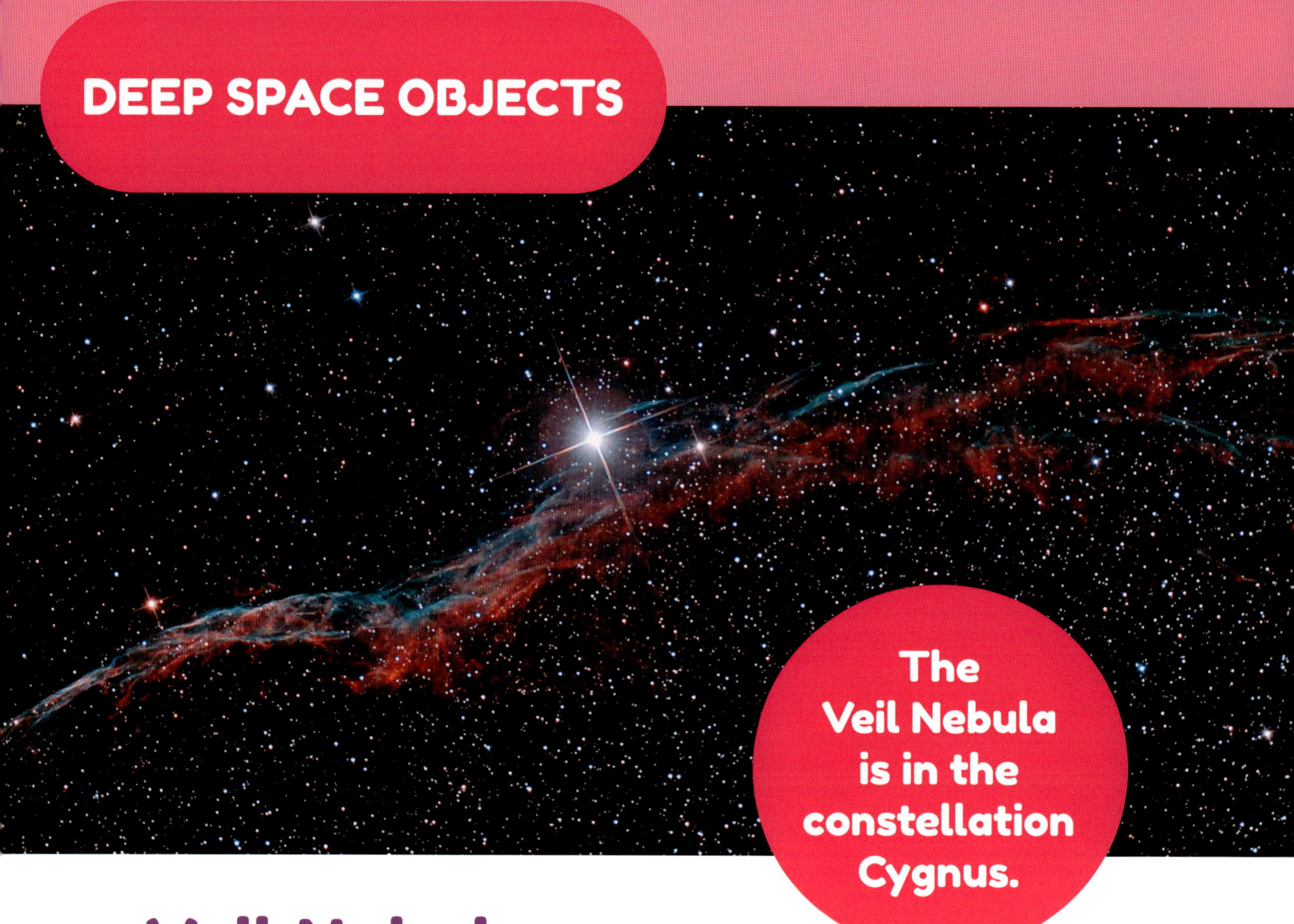

The Veil Nebula is in the constellation Cygnus.

Veil Nebula

The Veil Nebula formed when a star exploded more than 100,000 years ago. People need binoculars or a small telescope to see it. Some people think it looks like a wrinkled bedsheet.

A Pretty Picture

The Veil Nebula is popular among astrophotographers. The nebula's red and blue-green colors give it a beautiful appearance.

Cassiopeia A

Cassiopeia A also formed from an exploding star. People on Earth observed the explosion in the late 1600s. This nebula is found near the end of the *W* in the Cassiopeia constellation. Stargazers need a telescope to see it.

A NASA telescope captured this image of Cassiopeia A.

Eagle Nebula

- The Eagle Nebula is located in the constellation Serpens. This nebula is also known as M16.
- The Hubble Space Telescope has taken stunning photos of the Eagle Nebula. One famous photo is nicknamed "The Pillars of Creation."

The Eagle Nebula through a backyard telescope

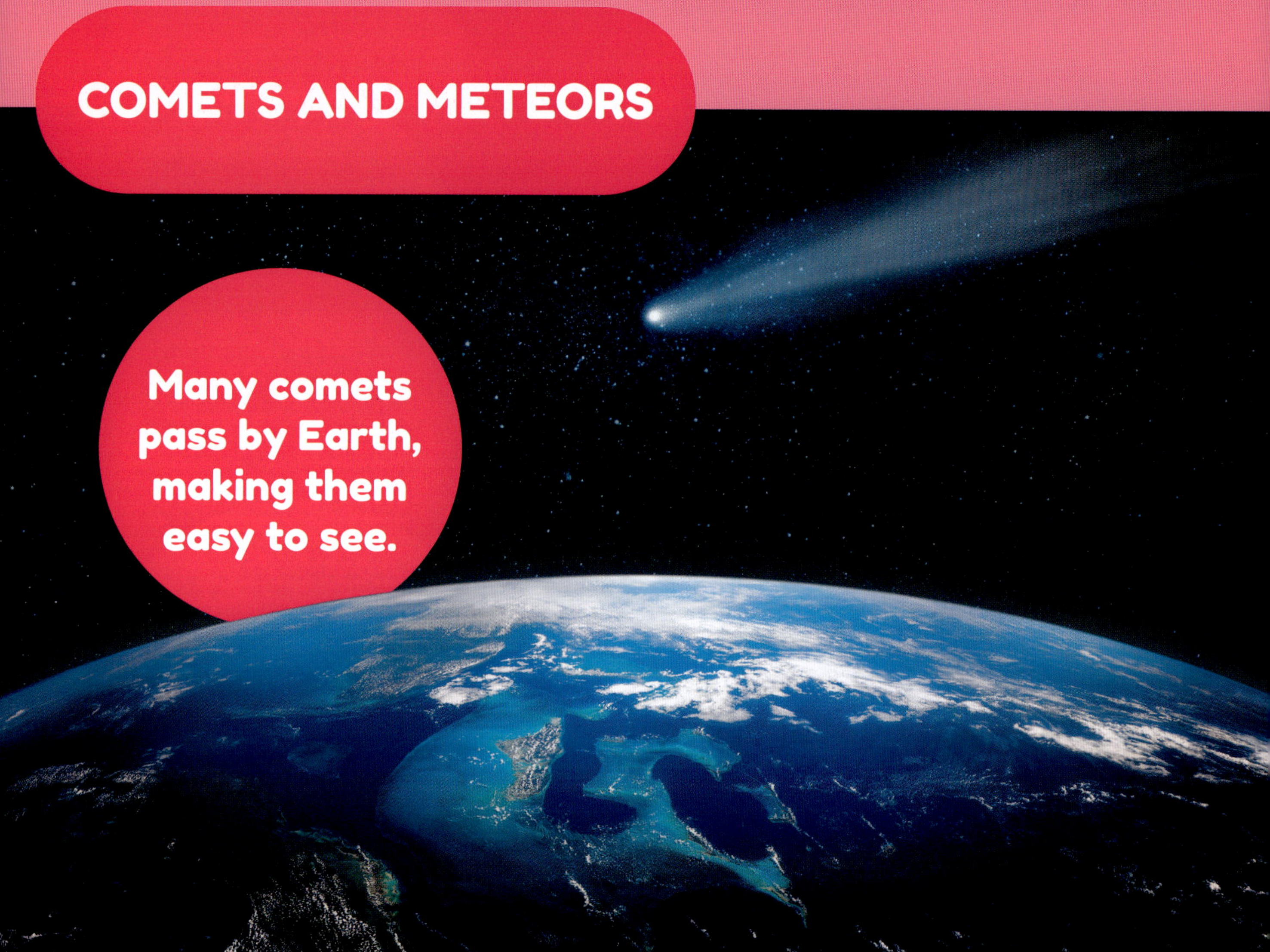

Many comets pass by Earth, making them easy to see.

What Are Comets?

Comets are made of dust, rock, and ice. These materials are left over from the early solar system. People on Earth can see comets as they get close to the sun. They look like fuzzy stars with tails. Comets can be several miles wide.

The Parts of a Comet

The frozen core of a comet is called its nucleus. The sun's heat melts part of the nucleus. This creates a cloud of gas and dust called a coma. As the comet moves toward the sun, material streams off it. Two tails form. One is blue and made of gas. The other is white and made of dust.

A comet's tails are far larger than its nucleus.

Heating Up

A comet heats up as it gets closer to the sun. The tails of gas and dust can stretch for millions of miles. Scientists think there may be billions of comets orbiting the sun.

Comets sometimes zoom past the planets as they approach the sun.

Comets spend most of their time as frozen objects far from the sun's warmth.

Moving Away

A comet loses its coma and tails as it moves away from the sun. The gas freezes. The comet stays frozen until it gets close to the sun again.

Stargazers and astronomers around the world watched as Halley's Comet appeared in 1986.

Halley's Comet

Halley's Comet is one of the best-known comets. It becomes visible from Earth every 76 years. Halley's Comet last passed Earth in 1986. It is expected to return in 2061.

Hale-Bopp

Another famous comet is the Hale-Bopp Comet. It came close to Earth in 1997. It was 1,000 times brighter than Halley's Comet. But Hale-Bopp won't reappear for a long time. It will be visible from Earth again in the year 4385.

Hale-Bopp's two tails can be seen in this 1997 photo.

Surprise Comets

Scientists do not always know when a comet is coming. NASA discovered the comet NEOWISE in March 2020. It came close to the sun just a few months later. The comet was so bright people could see it with the naked eye.

NEOWISE was discovered using the Wide-field Infrared Survey Explorer (WISE) space telescope.

People around the world watched for NEOWISE in the night sky.

Once in a Lifetime

NEOWISE will not pass Earth again for another 6,800 years. Long gaps like this make seeing a comet a special event. Some comets may be seen only once in a lifetime.

Millions of small meteors fall into Earth's atmosphere every day.

What Is a Meteor?

A meteor is a bright blaze of light in the night sky. It appears when a meteoroid enters Earth's atmosphere. In space, many rocks called asteroids orbit the sun. Meteoroids form when asteroids crash together and small pieces fly off.

Burning Up

Earth's gravity pulls meteoroids toward the planet. They enter Earth's atmosphere at high speeds. Meteoroids burn up as they hit the air. This creates bands of light.

FUN FACT!

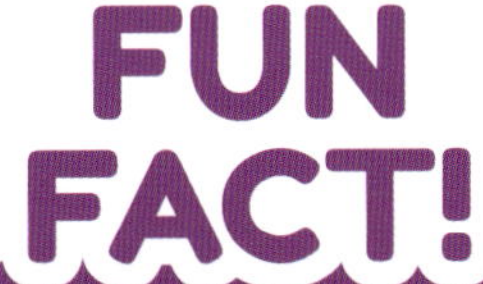

Especially bright meteors are called fireballs.

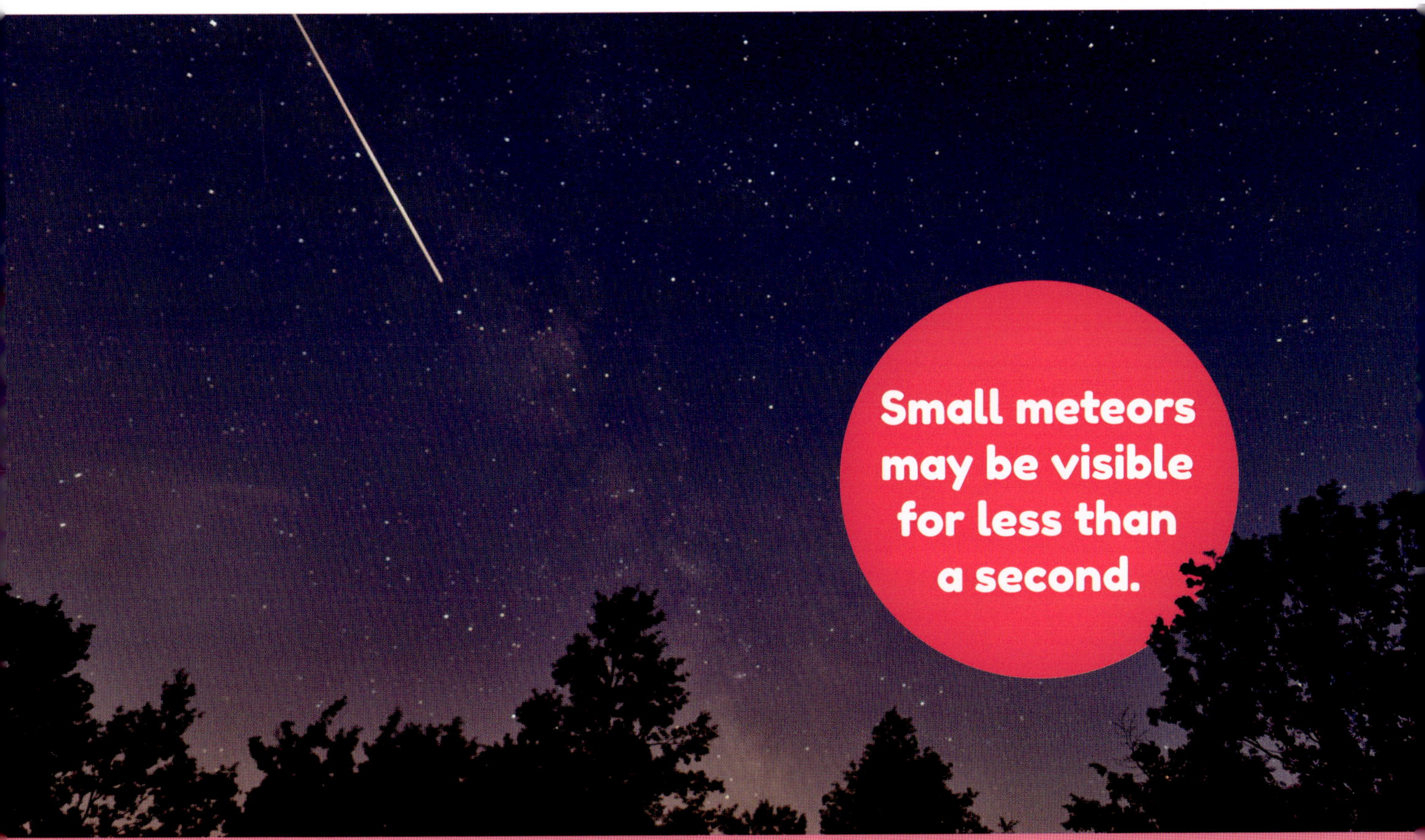
Small meteors may be visible for less than a second.

Not Really Falling Stars

Many people call meteors falling stars. Others call them shooting stars. This is because the meteors look like stars as they dart across the sky.

Meteors are easiest to see in places with very dark skies.

Earth's orbit takes it through several clouds of space rocks.

Meteor Showers

Meteor showers happen when many meteoroids enter Earth's atmosphere. These events happen at expected times each year. At these times, Earth moves close to a group of asteroids or a comet's tail.

A time-lapse photo shows many meteors from a Quadrantids shower.

Famous Meteor Showers

There are several major meteor showers. Stargazers can see the Quadrantids every January. The Lyrids happen each April. Some of these events last for weeks. But peak viewing times may be just hours long.

How They Get Their Names

Most meteor showers get their names from nearby stars or constellations. The Perseids are one of the best-known meteor showers. They occur near the constellation Perseus.

The Perseids come from the comet Swift-Tuttle.

GLOSSARY

agency
A part of a government that does a particular job.

astronomer
A person who studies space.

atmosphere
The gases that surround an object in space.

celestial
Related to the stars, planets, and other objects in space.

crater
A pit in the ground caused by the impact of an object.

gaze
To look at something for a long time with wonder or curiosity.

gravity
A force that objects have that pulls at other objects.

hemisphere
One half of Earth.

interstellar
Occurring between stars.

material
Matter.

meteoroid
A small rock traveling through space.

orbit
To follow a curved path around another object.

phase
One part of a natural cycle that something goes through.

solar system
The sun along with all the planets, moons, and other bodies that orbit it.

supergiant
A bright star that is bigger and hotter than the sun.

tilted
At an angle instead of straight.

TO LEARN MORE

More Books to Read

An Anthology of Stargazing. DK, 2025.

Bullard, Lisa. *The Planets*. Abdo, 2026.

Edwards, Sue Bradford. *The Moon*. Abdo, 2026.

Online Resources

To learn more about the night sky, please visit **abdobooklinks.com** or scan this QR code. These links are routinely monitored and updated to provide the most current information available.

PHOTO CREDITS

Cover Photos: Adobe Stock, front; Mikolaj Niemczewski/Adobe Stock, back

Interior Photos: Shutterstock Images, 1, 3, 4, 7, 8, 9, 13, 15 (top), 15 (bottom), 16, 17, 23 (top), 23 (bottom), 24 (top), 24 (bottom), 25, 29, 34, 36, 37, 38 (top), 38 (bottom), 39, 40, 41, 42 (top), 42 (bottom), 43, 44, 45, 46, 48, 49, 50, 53, 54, 56, 58, 60, 62, 66, 68, 71 (bottom), 79 (top), 79 (bottom), 80, 82, 84, 85, 86, 87, 88, 89 (top), 89 (bottom), 90, 91, 92, 94 (top), 97, 100, 102, 106, 108 (top), 110, 112, 113, 115, 121; David Carillet/Shutterstock Images, 5; Royal Astronomical Society/Science Source, 6, 57, 96; Max Alexander/Science Source, 10; John Chumack/Science Source, 11, 35, 77; Franck Legros/Shutterstock Images, 12; Ethan Miller/Getty Images News/Getty Images, 14; iStockphoto, 18, 47; NASA, 19, 69, 75, 78, 93 (top left), 93 (top right), 93 (bottom left), 93 (bottom right), 95, 104, 105, 107, 109, 110–111; Jung Yeon-Je/AFP/Getty Images, 20; Robert Goode/Shutterstock Images, 21; Pavel Gabzdyl/Shutterstock Images, 22; Jeff Dai/Stocktrek Images/Science Source, 26; Jojo Shaun/Shutterstock Images, 27; Daniel Chu Owen, 28; Alan Dyer/VW Pics/Science Source, 30, 31; Masahiro Suzuki/Shutterstock Images, 32; Mark Garlick/Science Source, 33; Cinematic Collection/Warner Bros./Alamy, 51; Iryna Shek/Shutterstock Images, 52; Science & Society Picture Library/Getty Images, 55; Science Source, 59; Jason Wells/Shutterstock Images, 61; Jurgen Ziewe/Shutterstock Images, 63; Babak Tafreshi/Science Source, 64; Jamie Cooper/SSPL/Getty Images, 65; Mariusz Klarowicz/Shutterstock Images, 67; Nowwy Jirawat/Shutterstock Images, 70; David Hajnal/Shutterstock Images, 71 (top); Damian Peach/Science Source, 72; New York Public Library/Science Source, 73; Damian Peach/Chilescope team/Science Source, 74; Tobias Roetsch/Future Publishing/All About Space/Future/Getty Images, 76; Visual China Group/Getty Images, 81; Tim Murphy/Shutterstock Images, 83; Manuela Durson/Shutterstock Images, 94 (bottom); Mustafa Bukulmez/Shutterstock Images, 98; Lukasz Pawel Szczepanski/Shutterstock Images, 99; Jan Kozak/Shutterstock Images, 101; Fabrizio Francione/USRA, 103; Kosong Tujuh/Shutterstock Images, 108 (bottom); Richard Bizley/Science Source, 114; Bettmann/Getty Images, 116; Education Images/Universal Images Group/Getty Images, 117; Adam Bencsik/Shutterstock Images, 118; David McNew/Getty Images News/Getty Images, 119; Vadim Sadovski/Shutterstock Images, 120; Benjamin Schaefer/Shutterstock Images, 122; Roger Harris/Science Source, 123; Juan Carlos Casado/starryearth.com/Science Source, 124; Makarov Konstantin/Shutterstock Images, 125